A MARINE FROM RENAULT

A MARINE FROM
RENAULT

An Alternative Start to a Career Path

Andrew J. Rickert

Archway Publishing books may be ordered
through booksellers or by contacting:

Archway Publishing
1663 Liberty Drive
Bloomington, IN 47403
www.archwaypublishing.com
1 (888) 242-5904

Because of the dynamic nature of the Internet, any web
addresses or links contained in this book may have changed
since publication and may no longer be valid. The views
expressed in this work are solely those of the author and do
not necessarily reflect the views of the publisher, and the
publisher hereby disclaims any responsibility for them.

Any people depicted in stock imagery provided
by Thinkstock are models, and such images are
being used for illustrative purposes only.
Certain stock imagery © Thinkstock.

ISBN: 978-1-4808-4401-8 (sc)
ISBN: 978-1-4808-4402-5 (e)

Library of Congress Control Number: 2017903081

Print information available on the last page.

Archway Publishing rev. date: 03/24/2017

CONTENTS

AUTHOR'S NOTE

This is a book about my actual experience on what I did in the US Marine Corp after leaving high school. This book provides a detailed description of my three years and three month experience in the Corps. This was my first adventure after graduating from high school and leaving my home in Renault, Illinois, and my family farm at age seventeen.

Many high school graduates, people who don't complete high school, and individuals who don't choose to further their education go from job to job simply to survive and sometimes without finding a suitable job, or they elect to do the unthinkable, like seeking fast money through crime. However, one can pursue various avenues after graduating from high school. College, technical school, apprenticeship in the trades, jobs, and so forth come to mind. If none of these is attractive or available, then perhaps the military may be advantageous to explore. The point is there are other avenues to consider when deciding on the proper path for the future. The purpose of this book is to demonstrate that there is a path to success after high school for individuals who may not be sure about what to do after graduation or who lack the financial resources to continue their education. This book is also for both men and women.

There is professional training in the military that is also useful in civilian life, though I was not fortunate to secure this professional training myself. Instead, they assigned me to the infantry (Fleet Marine Force) as a mortar man in the 1950s. This military experience was a valuable stepping-stone to my future based upon the discipline and teamwork approach instilled in me by the marines. Perhaps there are individuals who are apprehensive about joining the military. This is why I explain in detail my experience. My hope is that by sharing this, you may overcome any apprehension about the military as a choice.

I understand that combat duty is the biggest concern for anyone thinking about entering the military. This concern is certainly understandable. However, as citizens, we have the opportunity to help defend our country and protect our freedom. Likewise, the military has the responsibility to train and equip personnel to prevent, or at least reduce, casualties. You must remember that civilian casualties occur several times each day too, through crime, transportation, and occupational accidents.

My induction process into the marines and my journey from St. Louis, Missouri, to the Marine Corps Recruit Depot, Paris Island, South Carolina, in 1954, was during a time of heightened racial strife in the South. This was a new experience for me, as were the decisions I would have to make because of it. The shocking experience I encountered in my initial meeting with marine drill instructors was also overwhelming.

Boot camp was another exciting experience. During that period, I used a smoker's ingenuity to obtain additional smoking privileges on Sundays at church proceedings. I also experienced a stressful time with a medical situation while serving on mess duty. This is where discipline and teamwork was instilled in my mind. There also were humorous times as on the post-exchange visit when a recruit thought he could outsmart a drill instructor.

After boot camp, they assigned me to the Second Marine Division at Camp Lejeune, North Carolina, where I became a mortar man with the Sixth Marines. During this time, I was part of several amphibious landing maneuvers. Two of these were in Vieques, Puerto Rico, and Labrador; others were in several countries in the Mediterranean. It was during this time in the Mediterranean that I also faced a near-combat situation, which I will explain in detail.

After completion of active duty, I go into detail of my civilian life. I attribute most of my success in civilian life to the discipline and teamwork training I received from the marines. The training and life in the military opened my eyes to the many opportunities available that I would not have otherwise known. I also go into detail about my first job in civilian life as a mail clerk, the further training that was possible through the GI Bill, and the other circumstances that acted as a stepping-stone to further advancements.

I also write about my marriage to my wife, Bessie, and about how we raised our four daughters. I provide an account of my family's relocation to Denver, Colorado, and then back to St. Louis, where I entered the federal civil service. Later, we relocated to Battle Creek, Michigan, then finally to Alexandria, Virginia, and southern Maryland where I retired. While these were many moves, mobility is sometimes a valuable asset for success. Another aspect to consider on the road to success is to have a backup plan if the original career path fails. In my case, I pursued real estate sales as a backup plan.

Military experience was the stepping-stone to my civilian success. I hope this may assist individuals trying to decide on what to do after leaving high school. Just remember that life can be full of good things and welcomed surprises if you give it a chance.

Chapter 1

A HIGH SCHOOL CHAT AND BEYOND

"What in the world are you going to do when you graduate from high school?" Leroy asked me, a kid from Renault, Illinois.

"Gosh! I am not sure," I replied. "I suppose I have been thinking about joining the military."

"Andy, are you crazy?" Leroy yelled. "Who in the hell would want to do that? Only a fool would consider doing such a thing."

This conversation went on for a while at our high school, Saints Peter & Paul High School (now named Gibault High School) in Waterloo, Illinois. Saints Peter & Paul High School was a Catholic institution and was very strict on religious principles. Leroy was a very popular athlete, in addition to being a close friend of mine, but you would not have gotten the impression that we were good friends if you were listening in on our conversation. This was April 1954, with graduation staring us in the face in a little less than two months.

Some students were planning to go to college, some were getting jobs, and some were unclear on what to do next. In my case, I was formulating a plan that seemed controversial to some, though not to me. I was thinking about joining the military. I knew that my family did not have the financial resources to send me to college or trade school, and student loans, as far as I knew, were unheard of in 1954. Factory jobs were available, but listening to some of their employees' complaints about their jobs had turned me off from that idea.

The Korean War had just ended, and World War II was not that far in the past. I had listened to the stories of veterans from these wars and was impressed and influenced by them. I suppose that I paid little attention to the fact that the mission of the military was to protect our country in time of war, which could result in death or serious injury. When you are young, you too often think you are invincible.

Nevertheless, as a seventeen-year-old farm boy who had never traveled outside a fifty-mile radius of the farm, I felt I needed to travel away from Renault, and perhaps the military would provide me the opportunity. I also felt that there was not a bright future on the farm. Maybe military service would open my eyes on what to do the rest of my life.

Even though my friend Leroy argued strong and hard against my interest in joining the military service, it did not sink into my thick skull. I supposedly had a stubborn disposition when I had my mind made up, right or wrong. I might have inherited this from my mother's side of our family. Far be it from me to admit I was stubborn. Maybe I would have made a good baseball umpire.

The climate and attitudes toward the military were much different back in the 1950s than they are today. The Korean War had just ended, and people were still trying to recoup from the Great Depression and World War II. The attitudes of most people in that era were more toward patriotism than they are today. Everyone had the highest respect for the military. Recognizing I was a seventeen-year-old farm boy who grew up on a farm near Renault, Illinois the recent wars had a strong impact on my thinking. The military draft was still in operation, and men knew they would have to register once they turned eighteen. This was probably another and the greatest influence on me thinking about joining the military. I really did not want to wait for the draft. In addition, I wanted to choose which military branch to serve. However, because of my age, if I were going to enlist in the military I would need a parent's signature, which at the time was questionable. However, I kept planting the idea of enlisting to my parents in hopes that they would eventually see things my way. This was a fifty-fifty chance at best.

In early May 1954, I visited the different branches of the service recruiting offices and was very impressed with the US Marine Corps. The brochure on the Fleet Marine Force was most impressive. Seeing those marines climbing the nets on the side of a ship during an amphibious landing really caught my eye. I thought, *Hell this looks pretty simple. I am sure that I can do that.* The dress blue uniform also really caught my eye. *If I can wear one of those uniforms, I can really impress the girls.* I was convinced on the Marine Corps, but now I had to convince my parents.

The Marine Corps recruiting sergeant volunteered to join me in discussing this with my parents. My father would normally leave things like this up to my mother. However, he told me that if I was to leave home to join the military that I should not worry about the farm. He would manage all right and find help when needed. My mother had a brother who made a career in the navy and who did very well in our way of thinking. This was probably the main reason my mother agreed to sign the papers, and they did. I am sure that my parents were thinking of their struggles in trying to recuperate from the Great Depression, and perhaps it would be good for me to leave the nest, so to speak. This made me very happy, and it made the Marine Corps recruiting sergeant happy as well. Who knows? I might have made his recruiting quota for that reporting period. At the same time, I felt a little sad about leaving home.

Knowing the physical requirements of marines, I started running and doing pushups and other calisthenics. I was determined to become a marine regardless of what Leroy had to say.

I graduated from high school on May 31, 1954, and was in the Marine Corps on June 7, 1954. I know this did not leave much time for rejoicing after high school, but I wanted to get started. It might have been different if I had had a steady girlfriend, but I did not at the time. In fact, I did not even give my parents or friends time to arrange a going-away party. One thing for sure was that my friend Leroy could no longer talk me out of joining the military.

Chapter 2

THE ENLISTMENT AND INDUCTION PROCESS

The Marine Corps recruiting sergeant arrived at my house early on the morning of June 7, 1954. I was all ready to go. I had a small gym bag containing my shaving gear, underwear, and socks. My parents had sad looks on their faces, which made me a little sad too. I gave my parents a big hug, kiss, and promised to stay in touch by mail. Telephone services in those days were very archaic compared to todays.

We were on our way to East St. Louis, Illinois, for our first stop. This was the initial recruiting office we had to clear before reporting in to the Military Induction Center in St. Louis, Missouri. In addition, we had to pick up additional recruits. These recruits were all African American. This was my first exposure to African American people. There were no African

American people in Monroe County, Illinois where I grew up, as far as I knew. After World War II, President Truman integrated all races in the military, which in my opinion was the right thing to do. Prior to the president's action I am told that black and white military personnel were placed in different units. After a brief introduction to the recruiting staff in East St. Louis, we left for the Military Induction Center in St. Louis.

There was a lot of activity at the Military Induction Center. All of the military services initial processing for our area was at this center. It appeared to be mass confusion with all of the activity. A written test was our first challenge. I suppose this was for determining if we were literate. Next was our physical exam, which was rather thorough. They excused anyone who failed either exam. Our Marine Corps group passed both exams.

How these people at the Military Induction Center kept those records straight was amazing to me, with all of the apparent confusion. There were no computer systems as we have today. All of the record keeping chores were manual, which made things more prone to error. However, we were fortunate that we had no errors on our records, as far as we know.

The final item was the swearing-in, where we raised our right hand and repeated the oath, which made everything official. I wondered then if my friend Leroy would be proud of me entering the marines.

Once the swearing in was done, there was no backing out unless we were kicked out for some reason, such as insubordination, homosexuality, or bed-wetting. I really did not realize the full importance of the oath at the time, but as time went on, I soon learned. However, you must realize that I was rather naïve back then.

Everything at the induction center was now complete and we were ready to move to Paris Island, South Carolina, for boot camp. If we had enlisted in St. Louis, we would have moved to San Diego for boot camp because it would have been west of the Mississippi River. My group consisted of four African Americans and me. The marine recruiting sergeant instructed me to lead the group. He gave me the individual orders, train tickets, and meal tickets. The individual orders were for the receiving clerk at Paris Island. This was the first time in my life that I ever had to lead anyone or anything, but I accepted the responsibility and really had no choice, even though I was a little apprehensive on what to expect. In later years, I often wondered why they chose me to lead the group. Was it because of race? I will probably never know, but I hope that was not the reason.

The recruiting sergeant drove us to St. Louis Union Station and we boarded the train for Paris Island. In today's world, we would have flown there. However, in 1954, the railroad was the main means of transportation for this type of endeavor. Our first stop was Atlanta, Georgia, where we had a layover and a transfer to another train to Augusta, Georgia.

This was my first exposure to racial segregation. The restrooms were marked "Whites only" and "Colored only." The restaurants were marked the same way. I was from Monroe County, Illinois where there were no African Americans to my knowledge. As a result, this was a new experience for me. I did not realize it at the time, but there was a sign on State Route 3 near the Monroe County seat in Waterloo, Illinois, that read, "Negroes were not allowed after sundown". My religious training told me that all people were equal, and this is how I proceeded. I gave the meal tickets to the African Americans, and this worked out well. We then boarded the train for Augusta, Georgia, and everything was going smoothly.

While in Augusta, we waited for a bus to transport us to Beaufort, South Carolina, which was close to Paris Island. When boarding the bus, the African Americans in my group sat down in the front seats. The bus driver yelled, "Get your black a** to the rear of the bus!" What a shocker to us. Evidently, my African American peers from East St. Louis were not use to this type of treatment either. I started to follows them to the rear of the bus, and the bus driver said that I could stay up front. However, I did not. I joined them in the rear. This gesture seemed to please my African American friends, and I knew it was the right thing to do.

We arrived in Beaufort late in the evening, and low and behold, we had two Marine Corps drill instructors (DIs) waiting to greet us. I had never before heard such colorful language in all my life! They made us feel like we were the lowest of the low lives. A few recruits made wisecrack remarks, and they suffered from the DI's a** kicking.

"Put that damn cigarette out!" one DI yelled at a recruit. "You don't smoke until I tell you to smoke."

This is how recruits were treated. Now things perhaps have improved some. I was never so shocked in all of my life. I suppose this is one way of determining if you stood a chance of making it through boot camp. I was not the only one in shock. Most of the other recruits also were. They herded us onto a Marine Corps bus and transported us a short distance to the Paris Island Reception Center. You could have heard a pin drop on the bus. It seemed that all of the recruits were like me, wondering what they had done to deserve such treatment. This made me think, *was Leroy correct?*

Chapter 3

BOOT CAMP

It was getting late in the evening when we arrived at the Paris Island Reception Center. I guess the drill instructors (DIs) thought they had us under control, so they let us smoke a cigarette and made sure we put them out in a butt can. They then herded us into a barracks with upper and lower bunks, showed us where the head (Marine Corps terminology for a bathroom) was located, and bid us goodnight in a very hostile manner. Prior to bidding us good night, I handed my groups orders to the DI who gave them to the receiving clerk.

How anyone could sleep after going through this humiliating treatment rendered by these two DI's was beyond me and I will never know. I thought many times of my conversation with my friend Leroy. He appeared to be right in not wanting to join the military. When I settled down from this shocking experience, I am not ashamed to say that I actually started to shed a few tears, wondering what in the world a seventeen-year-old kid from a farm in Renault, Illinois, was getting into and why. I could not come to grips knowing that boot camp was going to last for ten to twelve weeks. Maybe I should have been a little more attentive to my conversation with Leroy a few months earlier. Maybe my stubbornness was starting to get the best of me. At the time, I really did not understand the purpose of this type of treatment, but a little later on, I knew that they were preparing us for combat behavior. If you could not take this kind of harassment and discipline, then you would not be of value, and in fact, you would be a hindrance in combat operations. Nevertheless, at this point, I felt that I had made a huge mistake.

The next morning, I awakened by a DI calling cadence as he marched a platoon of recruits on a parade field close to the barracks where we were sleeping. I was able to doze off a little that night, but it was a long way from a reasonable night's sleep. Then another DI came into our barracks and slammed a metal garbage can lid on the concrete floor to make sure everyone was awake by yelling, "Get your damn a** out of the sack and be ready for chow in thirty minutes!" There was not much time to dress and go to the head. By not shaving or showering, we were ready. He then herded us through a mess hall for breakfast. I could not eat much because of the shocking treatment we were receiving. I still could not realize what I had done. What caused me to be treated way?

After breakfast, the DI put us in a formation and permitted us to smoke by lighting the *smoking lamp*. This is the term used by the marines to permit smoking. He emphasized that no one could smoke until the DI lit the smoking lamp. He also told us we had to field strip the cigarette butts and showed us the procedure. The purpose of this was to keep the area free from cigarette butts. Most cigarettes back then had no filters. Most of them today have filters. I am not sure on what they do with the filters after fieldstripping.

The DI then herded us to the barbershop. There must have been a dozen barber chairs. Each chair had a barber waiting for the next recruit. There was no telling the barber how you wanted your haircut. All that you had to do was to sit in the barber chair and in about two minutes or so your hair was gone. I had heard from some veteran GIs that this was what they did to recruits, so this was not a shock to me. However, some of the recruits were not expecting this, and they were very disappointed in their new hairless style. I could understand the purpose of these haircuts to promote sanitation. Additionally these haircuts put everyone on equal footing regarding looks. I looked around at some of my fellow recruits and saw some sad faces, and others were angry about their haircuts. However, everyone had sense enough now to keep his mouths shut. We also joined up with additional recruits who had arrived before and after our group had, which made a platoon in size.

The next stop was the issuance of clothing. We received everything that was Government Issue (GI), but no dress blues. This was really a letdown to me. My dream world of impressing the girls was gone. You had to purchase these dress blues yourself if you wanted them, but not until you completed boot camp. The only exception would be for those assigned to sea or embassy duty. They issued dress blues to them after boot camp. We had to stencil our name on all underwear and utility garments. The garments requiring dry cleaning were also marked inside the collar on the shirts and inside the shoulder on the jackets. I suppose that the purpose of this was to prevent theft. At this point, the honesty of individual recruits was unknown. We were also issued dog tags (two) with a beaded chain and told to wear them like a necklace at all times. They had your name, military service, service number, and blood type. We were also issued a sea bag (also called a duffle bag by the Army and Air Force) to carry our clothing.

At this point, all of the basic boot camp entry processes were complete. We then saw the DIs who would work with us through graduation. These were two mean-looking individuals. If we thought the DIs that met us at Beaufort were strict and mean, compared to these two we were wrong. They made it clear that there were consequences for any screw-ups on our part. The DIs promised that we all would not graduate for various reasons. This started to worry me. The question of, what if I was one of those who did not make it to graduation? I would be a disgrace to the folks back home. This thought probably made me more determined than ever to succeed. There would be no smoking until one of them would light the smoking lamp. No one would wear the Marine Corps emblems until graduation. We were to address all non-recruits as "sir" and stand at attention while speaking. We would have mail call once a day and we had best write to our folks. If we wished to contact a chaplain, all we had to do was to request it from one of them. I could imagine asking one of these DI's permission to see the chaplain. We were not that naïve.

We were then marched to our barracks. The barracks were to be clean at all times. They were long, narrow, two-story frame structures with two rows of twin bunks (upper and lower) running down each side. There was one bathroom on each level. Each bathroom could accommodate about fifteen to twenty people at once.

Once we got to our barracks, we received more rules. Weekly church would be available for Catholics, Protestants, and Jews. Muslims and other denominations were not included. I do not think we had any of these other denominations in our platoon. We were never to leave the barracks alone. If we had a medical problem, the DIs would give us permission to go to *sickbay* (medical clinic). At this point, I would have to be next to death before I would have requested to go to sickbay from one of these DI's.

After that, we were marched to the mess hall. After chow, the DI would light the smoking lamp if everything were going well. If not, there would be no smoking. You would only be able to watch the DIs smoke and drool. They provided us with a bed and footlocker once when we returned to the barracks.

I soon learned that if you were with the group that marched to church, you received a smoke break before and after church services. The Catholics went first. Being a Catholic, I went with that group. About a half hour after we returned, the Protestants would march to church. After a couple of weeks, I decided to take advantage of the smoke breaks and joined the Protestant group too. In later years, my smoking may have caused me to be afflicted with chronic obstructive pulmonary disease (COPD). I also realized that this was sort of a sacrilegious stunt on my part to go to church only to satisfy my smoking habit. I did not realize at the time that I not only was contributing to a health problem but that my behavior was a spiritual disappointment because I was not seriously participating in the church services. This was particularly bad on my part because I had graduated from a Catholic high school and should have known and acted better.

The next step in the process was to sign out for a M1 rifle, padlock, and 782 gear items, which consisted of a helmet liner, pack, poncho, shelter half, cartridge belt, canteen, mess gear, first aid packet, and bayonet. We were marched to the supply room to obtain and sign for these items. Then we were marched back to the barracks and received instructions on how make our bed, which had to be done every time the bed was not in use. The next step was how to stow your 782 gear. We strapped our backpack and associated items on one side of the bunk end and our cartridge belt with bayonet fastened to the other side of our bunk end, with the helmet liner on top. All of the bunks had to be in a straight line.

The next item was how to stow items in your footlocker. A very specific process on how things were to be stowed in the footlocker was required. I had never seen such detail in positioning items and on housekeeping in my short life. The barracks floor and bathrooms had to be clean, swept and mopped daily as a minimum. They conducted daily inspection of the barracks. There would be periodic "junk on the bunk" inspections by laying out all of your issued clothing on your bunk in a specific order. You had best have the required amount of issued clothing and properly marked. If you did not have a reasonable explanation for anything missing, you could expect additional duty as a minimum for punishment.

The DIs then gave us the rules for taps (going to bed), which occurred 10:00 p.m., or 2200 hours in Marine Corps terminology. The DI would enter the barracks and call us to attention. You would stand at attention at the head of your bunk, and then he would say, *"Hit the sack,"* and everyone would jump into bed at the same time. Heaven forbid if you knocked off a helmet liner or something when you jumped into the top bed. This would cause additional punishment such as ten to twenty push-ups. This actually happened once to me. The DI would then turn off the lights.

Reveille would normally occur around 6 a.m., or 0600 hours, with the DI dropping a metal trash can lid on the concrete floor and yelling, "Reveille! Chow in forty-five minutes." You had best make it or go hungry until noon. I learned early on that you had best shower and shave in the evening because there was not enough time in the morning. After breakfast, we would assemble in formation and do calisthenics for thirty minutes or so, and then we would go to work on the day's agenda, which included a lot of drilling on the parade field in addition to classes on a variety of military subjects.

The DIs taught the cleaning and securing of the M1 rifle. This was a very important item for the military services because with a clean, operational rifle and ammunition, you are a lethal weapon against an enemy. Otherwise, you could be a detriment to yourself and others. They really emphasized that we needed to secure our rifles by locking them in the rifle rack. The DIs would check the rifle rack often for unlocked rifles. This never happened to our platoon, but I can imagine what would have happened if we were in violation. The penalty would have been more than push-ups, with additional duty added on as a minimum. It probably would have been additional duty for several days. Inspections by both the DIs and officers were looking for rust, pitted inside barrels, excessive oil, and lint. In addition, the wooden rifle stocks had to shine. We would accomplish this by rubbing the stock with linseed oil. After the redundant disassembling and assembling the M1 rifle, we could do it for the most part blindfolded. In addition to the rifle inspection, the DIs and officers were also looking for proper hair grooming, clean shaves, and shined shoes and brass when in dress uniform. In those days, the combat boots were not shined but simply cleaned.

The DIs now had us in position to instruct us on the various formation alignments and commands. You had best not screw up or you would have a DI kicking you in the pants. We would do hours upon hours of marching and executing the various commands. After a while, it became second nature to react to the various commands. In addition to marching, we had many classes on weaponry, the Uniform Code of Military Justice (UCMJ), infantry tactics, chain of command, military rank, and other subjects. They provided us with a UCMJ book. This book was very explicit in laying out the rules of conduct and the consequences for any violations.

During evenings and weekends, when we were off duty, we spent time washing clothes, shining shoes, cleaning our rifles, polishing brass, shining our rifle stocks, cleaning the barracks and writing letters. There were no radios or television to enjoy. They had us cut off from the outside world. The DIs continued to remind us to write home. I think the DIs were fearful that if your loved ones didn't hear from you, they would contact their congressman, who, in turn, would contact the office of the Commandant of the Marine Corps, and all hell would break loose because the DIs would be on the bottom of the chain of command, and they would have to answer why. Fortunately, our platoon was not guilty of this as far as I know.

The DIs was right in saying that, "all of you would not graduate from boot camp". Much to our surprise our platoon size reduced by three recruits. This happened after the first week in boot camp. Why this occurred, no one knew, but all three were gone. It could have been bed-wetting, homosexual behavior, other reasons, or even possibly their own request to leave. Homosexuals could not serve in the military services until recently. The "Don't Ask, Don't Tell" policy enacted by President Clinton provided a means for some homosexuals to serve. Now the restriction of homosexuals to serve in the military no longer exists.

While in boot camp, each platoon had to perform one week of mess duty. The cooking staff assigned each recruit to a duty station. They assigned me to the *scullery* (pots and pans) duty station. Evidently, the soap we used to clean the pots and pans must have been some powerful stuff. After a day or so, my hands had huge blisters. One of the cooks told me that I needed to go to sickbay. First, I needed to check with my DI. I hated to do this because I could imagine what the DI would say and call me a slacker or something worse. I had no choice. So I went to one of my DIs, and lo' and behold, he was very sympathetic and told me to go to sickbay immediately, which I did. The doctor painted my hands with some purple medicine and gave me a "no-duty slip" for the rest of the week. He also provided me with additional medicine to apply after showering. He told me to show the no-duty slip to my DI and to the cooking staff and report back to him on Friday. I went to the cook to inform him, and he was very apologetic. I knew what to expect when I was going to see the DI. He was going to call me everything but an American citizen. However, I could not believe it—he was also very sympathetic and told me to stick around the barracks, sweep the floor occasionally when I felt like it, smoke whenever I felt like it, write letters, and go to chow at my leisure. I could not believe that this DI was actually humane.

I went back to the doctor on Friday, and he released me. My hands finally healed in another week or so. The week of mess duty was over, so I went back to the barracks, and all was well that ended well.

By this time, the DIs had us pretty well under control. They threatened to take us on a midnight march for several miles if we screwed up. We would march through the swamps with full combat gear based upon the severity of the screw up. This got our attention. More than ever, we helped each other in preventing any screw-ups. Our platoon was operating as a team, and that is what the DIs wanted. I suppose this is where teamwork and discipline became part of my thinking.

The next "to-do" item was getting our pictures taken I suppose for public relations. The photos were for your hometown newspaper and parents, or next of kin. They marched us to the picture studio where we put on a dress blue coat and a white barracks cap and got an individual picture taken. Of course, we could not keep the uniform. They sent one copy of the pictures to the hometown newspaper and a copy to home. Once everyone had their picture taken, we were marched back to the barracks to continue our training.

After another week or so of training, it was time to spend a week at the rifle range. Based upon my rabbit and squirrel hunting on the farm, I felt that this would be a snap. This was a real experience. While some of our platoon was shooting, the remainder was working in the pits, pulling targets, and placing colored spotter disks in the bullet holes so the instructor of the shooter knew how to score it. We had to shoot from the standing, kneeling, and prone shooting positions. I soon learned that this was not a snap. When shooting in the prone, rapid-fire position, the objective was to obtain a small group of shots as opposed to a scattered group. I was shooting on target number nine. I remember the range master saying that the group on target number nine "*looked like corn scattered in buffalo s**t.*" This was proof that I did not do too well. However, overall things went well at the rifle range, so to speak. I wound up shooting Marksman, which was the lowest of the qualification categories.

We were over halfway through boot camp, and we were getting low on toiletries and cigarettes. The plan was to get one Post Exchange (PX) call around half way through boot camp. It was finally our turn. The DI marched us to the PX, which was about a mile away. This was in late July and very hot in Paris Island. The sand fleas were flying around in abundance. The DI told us that we should refrain from buying *pogey bait* (slang for candy and sweets). The term "pogey" originated with marines in China prior to World War II when Baby Ruth, Tootsie Rolls, and so forth, were part of their rations. Sugar was scarce in China, and the word for "prostitute" in Chinese roughly translated to "pogey." The term *pogey bait* applied because of those marines using the services of a prostitute during the China deployment. Frenchie, from Baltimore, was one of our more outgoing recruits and bought a pint of ice cream. He thought the DI did not see him. When we were ready to return to the barracks, the DI called us to attention and called Frenchie front and center. He told Frenchie to remove his helmet liner, place his ice cream on top of his head, and then place his helmet liner back on his head and then get back into formation. The DI marched us back to the barracks with Frenchie's ice cream melting down over his face and the sand fleas having a feast. This was somewhat funny, but similarly, we all felt a little sorry for Frenchie.

Our training continued to include gas assault training with gas masks, swimming, marching (which we called troop and stomp), and a variety of military classroom sessions. The day before graduation, we were marched to the supply facility to turn in our rifle and 782 gear items. The rumor was that the 782 gear issued to marines was throwaway gear by the US Army, as evidenced by the usage wear. I think that was just *scuttlebutt* (rumors) but who knows.

Graduation day finally arrived. Now we could pin on our Marine Corps emblems, which made us very proud, and soon we could claim to be marines. All of my earlier concerns about having made the wrong decision were gone. We assembled in formation and marched onto the parade ground wearing our dress uniforms. The military creases in our uniforms were razor sharp, and our shoes sparkled from their spit shine. The Marine Corps brass, and the parents and sweethearts of some of the recruits occupied the reviewing stand. We marched by the reviewing stand with the band playing the marine corps hymn, which made chills run up and down our backs with pride. Our Company Commander presented the National Defense Ribbon to each of us.

Unbelievably, the DIs started treating us like humans. We received orders for a ten-day leave. The Marine Corps designated me to serve in the Second Marine Division at Camp Lejeune, North Carolina. Finally, I could claim to be a marine. I was extremely proud just knowing that I made it through boot camp. What would Leroy say now? Graduating recruits did not receive a promotion to Private First Class (PFC) due to government budget constraints. Platoons graduating in my era did not receive the promotion. My monthly pay as a private stayed at $83.20.

I returned home on my ten-day leave by bus. In today's environment I would have flown. Everyone was glad to see me, and the reverse was true for me. They were all happy to hear of my experiences thus far in the Marine Corps. Likewise, I was happy to receive all of the local news and rumors. I was unable to see my friend Leroy. When my leave was about to end, I left home by bus for my assignment at Camp Lejeune.

Chapter 4
ASSIGNMENT

I arrived at Jacksonville, North Carolina, and took a Marine Corps bus a short distance to the Camp Lejeune Reception Center. There were other marines on the bus from boot camp, some of whom I knew. You could tell the ones reporting in from boot camp by their short hair, slick sleeves (no stripes) on their uniforms, and the sea bag with all of their uniforms and belongings. Even though I had no reason to get that boot camp feeling of inferiority upon entering Camp Lejeune, but I did. Perhaps it took a little time to adjust my thinking that I was no longer in boot camp.

I reported in to the receiving area and they assigned me to Dog (now Delta) Company, Second Battalion, Sixth Marines, and Second Marine Division. The Fifth and Sixth Marines wore the French Fourragere. The French Government had awarded the French Fourragere to the Marine Corps for heroics in WWI in such battles as Belleau Woods and others. We call them "pogey ropes." Wearing the pogey rope on the marine green uniform instilled even a greater sense of pride. Why they chose the term *pogey rope* for the French Fourragere is beyond me because it had nothing to do with Chinese prostitutes. They then transported me to my unit. All of a sudden, I started feeling human again. The marines whom I was associated with now were courteous, polite, and rather humorous. I suppose the days of boot camp were starting to erode in my mind.

I was welcomed by the first sergeant, who was a master sergeant and called "*Top*," which is the colloquial name given to first sergeants. He assigned me to the 60MM Mortar Section. Top also introduced me to the company technical sergeant, referred to as the "*gunny*." The gunny was the one who really ran the day-to-day operations in the company. First, the 60MM mortar section personnel welcomed me. Then, the personnel in the rocket launcher section welcomed me. Together these two sections made up a platoon.

The marines called the 60MM mortar a "piss tube." I suppose this is because it resembles a urinal when in the firing position.

The Company Clerk assigned a bunk and footlocker to me and provided me with bed sheets, a wool blanket and the like. They briefed me on the duty roster and company policies. The Battalion supply sergeant issued me a M1 rifle and 782 combat gear items. Unlike boot camp, everyone treated me with dignity and respect. They instructed me on the process for formations and chow. We marched to the mess hall for all meals on weekdays and until normally noon on Saturday. We could straggle to chow on weekends starting at noon on Saturday. Corporals would be at the head of the chow line. Sergeants would straggle to chow at their leisure. Staff noncommissioned officers (NCOs) straggled to chow and had their own section in the mess hall. The Staff NCOs did not go through the chow line and had dishes instead of metal trays. Officers had their own dining facilities.

The staff NCO in charge of the mortar and rocket platoon assigned me to a squad in the 60MM mortar section. I trained on the 60MM mortar and started out as an ammunition carrier. We ran drills on speed and accuracy setting up a mortar to fire. We applied particular attention to the settings on the sight and firing increments required on the mortar round for a given distance. The search and traverse requirements were emphasized. We trained on how to support the rifle platoons as a forward observer who would direct the line of fire for the mortar target areas in support of the rifle platoons. This is where teamwork instilled in us in boot camp became extremely important.

We had to take our turn on battalion guard duty during off-duty hours, which was not that often. Privates and PFCs would perform the actual guard duty and be supervised by a sergeant of the guard and a second lieutenant who was the officer of the day (OD). The sergeant of the guard and OD would occasionally go around and check on the guards walking the assigned posts to make sure everything was secure. I suppose that the main reason was to make sure the assigned guard was walking his post and not sleeping. The guards walking the posts would be there for two hours and then be relieved by a replacement.

We had periodic rifle inspections by the company commanding officer (CO) and occasionally by the battalion CO. Every few months, we would have a "junk on the bunk" inspection. I felt extremely honored when our battalion executive officer performed the inspection because he was a Medal of Honor recipient from his heroics in World War II.

While in the infantry and fleet marine force (FMF) we did quite a few field exercises and bivouac operations. Our shelter halves that were used to make up our bed role was camouflage brown on one side and camouflage green on the other side. If you did not pay close attention to the bivouac orders and rolled your blanket role with the wrong color, you would wind up having to redo it. This is where the saying, "green side out" or "brown side out," originated and became sort of a joke between fellow marines. The same process also applied to helmet covers. Unlike boot camp, where we only had helmet liners, here we also had the actual helmet. The Marine Corps had us equipped for combat in very short notice.

There are four names given to marines. First, there was *leatherneck*, which went back to the days of fighting pirates. The term leatherneck is from leather neckbands worn in the late 1700s to protect marines from the slash of swords while fighting pirates. Second, there was *jarhead*, which originated from the "high and tight" haircut that many marines have, which made their head look as though someone placed a jar on top of their head and the hair cut around it. Third, there was *gyrene*, a term made by combining "*GI*" with *marine* to make *gyrene*. Last was *devil dog*, which originated from the German high command saying that marines were of storm trooper quality from their service in World War I.

The battle cry for the marines is "oorah." The motto for them is "semper fi", or Semper Fidelis, which means "always faithful."

The Marine Corps emblem is very special to marines, and it identifies and is the symbol for the mission and purpose of the Marine Corps. The three components are the eagle, which is the symbol of the United States, and is the one part of the emblem that readily associates the Marine Corps with the United States. The eagle proudly carries a streamer in its beak that bears the motto of the Corps: *Semper Fidelis*. Then there is the globe, which signifies the worldwide commitment of the Marine Corps and its areas of responsibility. Marines serve in any climate or place. Last, is the anchor, whose origin dates back to the founding of the Marine Corps in 1775 and represents the amphibious nature of the marines' duties, emphasizing the close ties between the Marine Corps and the US Navy.

We all had the opportunity to go on liberty during off-duty hours. This was if we did not screw up and have our liberty card pulled. We would normally wear civilian clothes on liberty. We would go to towns surrounding Camp Lejeune, like Jacksonville and Wilmington. At that time, only a few marines had cars. Those who did would go a little further. There was always a duty NCO assigned to off-duty hours in each company. The duty NCO would sign you out and give you your liberty card. The liberty card showed that you were on authorized liberty. When you returned you would check in and give the liberty card back to the Duty NCO. We used the same process when we went on extended leave in addition to having orders authorizing leave. If you failed to return from liberty or leave on the date and time specified on the orders you were *"absent without leave* (AWOL)". This is a court-martial offense and punishable by such things as reduction in rank and time in the *brig* (jail), depending on the severity of the offense as determined by the company CO or executive officer.

In any group of people, there will occasionally be disagreements. Perhaps not always, but in many cases, when marines disagreed adamantly, they would unofficially settle their disagreement with a fistfight in a secluded area such as in the woods or behind a building where there would be no witnesses. If this resulted in visible, physical wounds such as a black eye, the wounded person would claim to have accidently tripped over a footlocker and fallen, or some other similar concocted story. Once this fistfight occurred the two combatant marines shook hands and everyone seemed happy. I am not sure whether marines of today unofficially settle disagreements in this manner.

There were women marines also stationed at Camp Lejeune. Women marines were all housed separately from the men. They performed mostly in noncombat duties at that time. This has changed in recent years in that women marines are moving more toward combat-related duties. As mentioned earlier, marines have their own vernacular for many things and situations. In the case of women marines, male marines referred to them as "*broad a** marines*" (BAMs). When they would see a woman marine, they would say, "Rabbit, BAM, BAM," as if they were rabbit hunting. This is the way it was during my tenure in the corps in the 1950s.

I also tried to go to mass on Sundays, as was emphasized by my parents and by my high school training from the nuns. The chapel was right across the street from our barracks. Generally, I performed this routine while at Camp Lejeune. This applied both before and after amphibious maneuvers elsewhere. Maneuvers conducted on Sundays would have a field alter set up for Catholic mass and Protestant services.

Chapter 5
FIRST MANEUVERS IN VIEQUES, PUERTO RICO

The Marine Corps conducted amphibious training and field maneuvers in Vieques, Puerto Rico, for several years during my tenure in the marines. They conducted these maneuvers in the early months of the year, normally February through May. Vieques is a small island in the Caribbean, approximately twenty-two miles long and approximately four-miles wide at the widest point near the main island of Puerto Rico. The US Navy used about half of the island for naval gunfire training on one end of the island and storage and radar on the other end. The Marine Corps being part of the Navy used the island for amphibious training and field maneuvers. The Puerto Ricans also used the entire island when not in use by the Navy and Marine Corps for grazing by their livestock. The Navy and Marine Corps have discontinued using Vieques in recent years. Since then, Vieques has become a very popular tourist attraction and rated as one of the best in the Caribbean.

Our company prepared for these maneuvers in the Caribbean by filling our sea bags with our uniforms, personal items, and the company items such as administrative equipment and material, personnel records, and other miscellaneous property. They setup a separate staging area for these items. They transported them separately to the ship. They transported us to Moorhead City, North Carolina, by *deuce and half (two-and-a-half-ton) trucks* to embark on the troop transport ship for our journey to Vieques. This was very exciting to me, being my first amphibious landing. If I could accomplish this, then I could claim to be a true marine, regardless of what my high school friend Leroy might have said.

This was about a five-day journey on the amphibious transport ship. During the day, we would have training sessions and do calisthenics as best we could. The navy personnel would be busy operating and maintaining the ship. Often times, we would be in the way of the navy personnel trying to do their job cleaning the deck, and as a result, they would "accidently" turn the hose on us. This really did not cause retaliation because we knew we were probably in the wrong by intentionally being in their way. At night, we often had a movie or we would go up to the main deck and smoke, watch the stars, and shoot the breeze. The chow was good too. I particularly liked their creamed chipped beef and toast we would occasionally have for breakfast. The marine slang for this was "s**t on the shingle." The navy used chipped beef for this, which I preferred to the ground beef the marines used.

We finally reached our destination offshore at Vieques. We were to make an amphibious landing on landing craft boats from the amphibious transport ship instead of on the amphibious tractors (AMTRACS), had we been on a landing ship tank (LST). They staged our sea bags separately and transported our sea bags and company gear separately to our tent area. This was my first amphibious landing. We boarded the landing craft by climbing down a net. We had to lower the heavier gear, such as our mortars, by rope. The first person in the landing craft would receive a rope that was sling tied to the mortar and would hold the mortar away from the ship to prevent damage. Marines held the net away from the ship's side in order for the marines to climb down properly. Fortunately, the sea was rather calm. This is difficult to do with rough seas. Teamwork, again, played an important role.

This was my first amphibious landing, and what an experience! This in no way mirrored my impression obtained from the brochure at the recruiter's office. This was not easy, but it gave me a further sense of pride thinking that I was doing the same type of effort done by marines in years gone by. Such heroic landing efforts by marines in the South Pacific during World War II, in such places as Tarawa, Guadalcanal, Saipan, Guam, and Okinawa, were in the back of my mind. The famous raising of the US flag on Mount Suribachi on Iwo Jima also came to mind. All of this ran through my mind, justifying why I was in the marines. Leroy probably would not have felt this way. I also thought of the army landing on D-Day during World War II off the coast of France where the ocean was much rougher than here in the Virgin Islands.

You had to be very careful in leaving the landing craft from the sides of the ramp to prevent having your foot damaged by the ramp jamming your foot against the beach. This would have meant broken bones for sure. Once we were ashore, we marched to the tent area where we would live for the next couple of months. Each tent would accommodate six people. We had folding cots with air mattresses to sleep on. The air mattresses did not stay inflated very long, which caused us to do the best we could with what we had. There was a mess tent for the battalion and bathroom tents with showers, toilets, and shaving areas. We were in the Caribbean, so at least the weather was warm.

Every day, except Sunday, we were in the field running a variety of maneuvers. We practiced our mortar utilization techniques, and on occasion would run joint maneuvers with the rifle platoons in our company. A person in our mortar section would join the rifle platoons and perform forward observer duties, calling in the range and directions requiring mortar support to include search (vertical) and traverse (horizontal) actions.

In addition, we did occasional live firing with our mortars. This bothered me some because of the occasional dud (a round not exploding). There were some horses running around in the area of our live firing that were not rounded up by the Puerto Ricans prior to our arrival, and I was fearful of a horse stepping on a dud and causing an explosion. I never experienced this, but I felt it could happen. I did report this concern to my platoon sergeant and platoon leader and they assured me that this would not happen because of demolition people retrieving and exploding the duds after we left the area. The gunny also chimed in and provided further assurance.

You would think that there would be snakes on the island of Vieques, but there were none. This was because of importing the mongoose many years earlier to Vieques. The mongoose was a small, ferret-like animal that was very fast and killed all of the snakes in Vieques over the years. No one really liked snakes, so the mongoose was certainly an appreciated species.

There is a small village on the island of Vieques named Isabel Segunda. There were a few souvenir shops, food places, and of course, saloons (or *slop shoots* in marine slang). They authorized us to go there on liberty occasionally. We had no refrigeration in our tent area, so we would normally bring back items like pepperoni that did not require refrigeration.

I had the opportunity to visit St. Thomas, Virgin Islands, after about a month into our Vieques maneuver for a little rest and recuperation (R&R). This was very enjoyable and enlightening to see how the residents lived. St. Thomas appeared to be an excellent place to vacation. However, my stay was too short for a vacation. There were historic buildings, including a 1679 Danish watchtower called Blackbeard's Castle as a reference to the area's pirate history. Unfortunately, I had to return to my unit in Vieques.

At the conclusion of our maneuvers in Vieques, we boarded our troop ship by climbing the nets. They staged and loaded our sea bags separately on the ship. On our way back to Moorhead City, North Carolina, we had port calls for a couple of days in Santo Domingo, Dominican Republic, and at Port-au-Prince, Haiti. This experience was much different from my visit to St. Thomas in that it was very depressing to see the deplorable conditions in which some of the native people had to live. Touring these places was very interesting and made us so thankful that we were Americans living in better conditions when compared to them. When we arrived in Moorhead City, there was deuce-and-a-half trucks waiting to transport us back to Camp Lejeune.

Shortly after returning from Vieques, Puerto Rico, they promoted me to private first class (PFC). Now I was earning $85.80 a month. What a raise in pay! This made me very happy, and I could not wait to get my PFC stripes sewed on my uniforms. They could no longer call me a slick sleeve or a boot. A boot meant that you were new to the corps and had just graduated from boot camp. In addition, anyone with a higher service number than you, right or wrong, was a boot to that individual. There is nothing wrong with being a boot. It merely meant that you had less seniority than someone who had a lower service number.

Shortly after returning from Vieques, they promoted me to assistant gunner in our 60MM mortar section. My personal weapon would no longer be the M1 rifle but a .45-caliber pistol. I turned in my M1 rifle, cartridge belt, and bayonet that they issued and then issued me a pistol belt and holster. They did not issue the 45-caliber pistol until you were on a maneuver or assigned a duty such as prison chaser that required a firearm. As assistant gunner, I had to help carry the mortar, and as such, could no longer carry the M1 rifle. The gunner and assistant gunner, both armed with .45-caliber pistols, carried the 60 MM mortar, site, and aiming stakes. The mortar was broken down into three main components, the based plate, tube, and bipod. Normally, one would carry the bipod and aiming stakes and the other, the base plate and tube. The gunner would also carry the mortar site that was in a leather case attached to his pistol belt.

Our training at Camp Lejeune continued using the same routine as before the Vieques maneuver.

Chapter 6
LABRADOR MANEUVERS

Winter was approaching in the fall of 1955, and cold weather maneuvers in Labrador were scheduled. They issued us cold-weather gear. We also participated in cold-weather training sessions. I really was not a fan of the cold, but I knew we had to be prepared. When the national situation was such and we would be required to fight somewhere in the world that was cold, such as it was in Korea we had to be ready. They transported us to Moorhead City by bus. I suppose the company CO felt that it was a little too cold to ride in deuce-and-a-half trucks. We did not take our sea bags because this maneuver was only going to be for about two weeks in duration.

We boarded our ship, which was a LST. This ship was different from the amphibious troop transport we were on for the Vieques maneuvers. The LST was flat bottom, and the bottom deck was loaded with AMTRACS. We left the dock and were on our way to

Labrador. The seas were rough in the north Atlantic. The ship continually went up and down very hard, which made you wonder if it would break in two. I became very seasick along with several others. The smell of diesel fuel in the berthing areas was bad. The navy personnel were constantly welding, which made you wonder if the ship was breaking up. I had to lie in my rack (name for bunk) for three days. My friend from Louisiana brought me crackers from the mess deck to eat. This type of teamwork kept me alive, or at least I thought it did. I started to recover a day or so before we arrived at Labrador.

On the day of the landing, we boarded the AMTRACS in full combat gear as the ship's captain lowered the ramp on the bow of the ship. The AMTRAC drivers started their engines, and then one by one they drove off the ships ramp into the ocean. The AMTRACS would sink below the surface and eventually come up to the surface and then onto shore. What a relief from the anxiety when our AMTRAC surfaced. The AMTRACS had another name, "iron coffins" by marines. I suppose the fear of the AMTRACS not surfacing once they sunk below the surface was the reason. I doubt if Leroy would have enjoyed this. We departed from the AMTRACS on the beach and marched to our bivouac area. There, we pitched tents with a friend, using our shelter halves, brown side out, tent poles, and pegs. We called these tents, "pup tents." We experienced several inches of snow, and it was very cold. Our food consisted of meal, combat, individual rations (or "C-rations") from World War II. We had Sterno fuel cans to heat our rations, which worked out fairly well.

This cold weather brought to mind the heroics performed by marines during the Korean conflict at the Chosin Reservoir, for an example. The actions of marine legend Chesty Puller also came to mind. Major General Puller was a marine's marine. The sacrifice we were making in our training exercise was minor compared to what these marines had to endure at the "Frozen Chosin".

We ran maneuvers during the day. At night, we slept. However, we had to perform guard duty during the night. One person in the platoon would stand guard duty for one hour. Under normal conditions, you would serve two hours, but due to the cold weather, we only had to serve one. Slick sleeves (privates) and PFC's performed the guard duty chores. They scheduled me to perform this duty from 1–2 a.m., or 0100–0200 in marine terminology, on the first night. Prior to retiring that evening, a corpsman stopped by and gave me a small bottle of brandy to help warm me up while on guard duty. I learned very fast that you needed to stay in good relationship with the corpsmen. The corpsmen were navy personnel assigned to the marines. They wore marine uniforms with navy rank insignia on their sleeves. Corpsmen were very compassionate people tending to our medical needs. This demonstrated again the value of teamwork.

At the end of three days of maneuvers, we marched back to the beach and boarded the AMTRACS for our return to the ship. This Labrador cold weather training maneuver and my Vieques experience, gave me a real sense of pride, and the feeling that now, more than ever, I was a true marine. What would Leroy say now?

Our return back to Moorhead City was uneventful. We did notice calmer waters as we proceeded south. When we arrived at Moorhead City, the busses were waiting to transport us back to Camp Lejeune.

We continued our normal duties at Camp Lejeune. They promoted me to gunner, which made me happy. I retained my personal weapon as a .45-caliber pistol. We received word that we would be having another maneuver in Vieques starting in February of 1956.

I took a ten-day leave to be with my parents and family over the Thanksgiving holiday in 1955. I had a very enjoyable time visiting, especially enjoying my mother's cooking, but I was anxious to get back to Camp Lejeune and start preparing for our next maneuver at Vieques. Unfortunately, I again missed meeting my high school friend Leroy, even though I made several attempts.

Chapter 7

SECOND MANEUVER IN VIEQUES, PUERTO RICO

Our second trip to Vieques was very similar to the first trip. The routine used for transporting our sea bags, company equipment and personnel records stayed the same. We all were familiar with the routine, and everything went well as we once more occupied our tents. The maneuvers were very similar in the beginning to the ones on the previous Vieques maneuver.

The marine corps is very strict on personal hygiene. I am sure the other services are too. An individual that I heard of from another company within our battalion was not keeping clean as expected by the Marine Corps. I understand that after several counseling sessions in hopes of correcting the problem resulted in no change in his personal hygiene. They contacted the company gunny on this matter. The gunny told them "you boys know what to do." This meant a blanket party, whereby several marines would cover his face with a blanket when he was sleeping, carry him to the shower, and give him a shower with a scrub brush. This was not an easy chore, but something that everyone felt needed to happen. This resulted in a positive change. I doubt if similar techniques to correct personal hygiene problems are common today, but maybe they are.

About midway through this maneuver, they authorized me to spend a couple of days in San Juan, Puerto Rico on R&R. I flew on a small cargo plane, which gave me the scare of my life. This was the first time in my life flying in a plane. Once airborne, I noticed fire coming off one of the engines. Fortunately, it was only a short distance from Vieques to the San Juan airport. We made it safely, and they immediately extinguished the fire. This was not an enjoyable flight. After a while, I recovered from my fear and was able to continue my R&R. I had a pleasant time in San Juan, sightseeing and shooting the breeze with the Puerto Ricans who could speak English. The cobblestoned streets of Old San Juan were very interesting, as were the colorful Spanish colonial buildings. After the two days in San Juan, I returned to Vieques on a flight without a scare, which I appreciated.

Shortly after returning, they informed me that I would be participating in a trial exercise on the use of helicopters in combat. Helicopters were used successfully by marines in the Korean War, especially in evacuating the wounded, transporting supplies, and general transport missions. Now, the thinking was to use helicopters more in a combat role in initial landings and assault missions. I, and a few other marines, made up a small group to go aboard a small aircraft carrier, the USS Siboney, which housed the helicopters and participated in ship-to-shore maneuvers.

Unfortunately, this only lasted for a few days. While we were on the aircraft carrier, we could not believe the good food we had: steak, real milk, real eggs, ice cream, and the like. I suppose that all good things have to come to an end eventually. The maneuvers were successful, if you recognize that the helicopters back then were not as sophisticated as they are today. They transported us back to our unit to continue our normal maneuvers.

We completed the Vieques maneuvers and boarded the ship for our return to Camp Lejeune. We had a port call in Havana, Cuba, which was very interesting. We were there through May Day, 1956. Dictator Batista was still in power. The Cuban revolution was not yet at full strength, which would bring Fidel Castro into power. The short time that we were there we were able to tour the city and even tour a rum producing facility where we consumed a few samples. Havana was a beautiful city and I hoped that someday I could return on vacation.

After leaving Havana, we returned to Moorhead City and boarded the deuce-and-a-half trucks to return to Camp Lejeune where we continued our normal routine. The next major effort was the rifle range. This is an annual exercise for the most part, whereby everyone in the FMF shot the M1 rifle for qualification. In addition to the M1 rifle, I had to qualify with the .45-caliber pistol since the .45 was my personal weapon as gunner on a 60MM mortar. I qualified as sharp shooter on the M1 and expert on the .45. I probably would not have done as well with the .45 if it had not been for the range instructor. He saw that I was bucking my shots, which meant that I was anticipating the shot to fire, and as a result, this caused me to jerk my pistol upward. To remedy this, the range instructor had me squeeze the trigger so that I would not know when the round would fire. This resulted in me becoming a shooting expert with the .45. Now I had two medals to wear on my dress uniforms: a sharp shooter medal for the M1 and an expert medal for the .45.

Shortly after completing the rifle range effort, our company went on rifle range duty at Camp Perry, Ohio, in support of the National Rifle Association (NRA) rifle matches. They transported us to Sandusky, Ohio by train and we moved to Camp Perry by bus.

Camp Perry is located on the shores of Lake Erie. They housed us in former prisoner of war (POW) huts from WWII. German POW soldiers previously occupied these huts. They would accommodate four people per hut, which was comfortable during these summer nights. It probably would not have been this way in the winter due to the cold weather near the Great Lakes.

The NRA hosted a welcoming party for our benefit at the Cedar Point Amusement Park near Sandusky, which was very nice. This gave us an opportunity to meet the girls, and that we did. We had to hitch hike rides to the various towns when on liberty, which was very easy when you wore your uniform. The people in this part of the country showed great respect to the military. Normally the first car that passed you would stop and give you a ride. Things have changed over the years and I realize that this for the most part is unheard of in today's environment.

Our job with the NRA was to operate the targets and keep score. We were very familiar on how to perform both of these functions. The shooters were all civilians with various types of rifles. These shooters had some wonderful-looking rifles, which made me very envious. I was comparing them to our M1 rifle, which was not fair because the M1 would serve for combat operations. The shooters rifles probably would not withstand combat operations.

During our stay at Camp Perry, I had the opportunity to attend a professional baseball game in Cleveland between the Indians and Tigers. This brought back memories of my younger years when relatives would take me to see the Cardinals and Browns (now the Baltimore Orioles) play at Sportsman Park in St. Louis. Our Camp Perry duty lasted for about forty-five days, and then we boarded the train back to Camp Lejeune.

We continued our normal duty routine at Camp Lejeune. They promoted me to Corporal, which made me happy. This brought my monthly pay up to $99.37. This not only put a few more dollars in my pocket, but I also could go ahead in the chow line as a noncommission officer. I was so proud to have corporal stripes sewed on my uniforms. In addition, this meant that if I purchased dress blues, I would have the red stripes down the outer legs of the blue trousers, indicating that I was an NCO.

My next assignment was to NCO school for two weeks at Montfort Point, which was part of Camp Lejeune. Upon completing NCO school and returning to my unit, I was in for a big surprise. My recruiting sergeant two years earlier became my platoon sergeant. There was probably only one chance in many that this could have happened, but it did. My friends told me that now I could get even with him for recruiting me, but I immediately discarded that thought. He was a great platoon sergeant and never showed any partiality to me because he had been my recruiting sergeant.

They assigned me to the position of squad leader responsible for one of three mortars and the personnel consisting of three ammunition carriers, a gunner, and assistant gunner. I no longer used the .45 as my personnel weapon and they issued me a M1 rifle and cartridge belt with bayonet after turning in my pistol belt and holster.

Chapter 8

MEDITERRANEAN CRUISE

I received word in December 1956 that our battalion was to go on a Mediterranean cruise in late January of 1957. The purpose of this cruise was to provide an amphibious task force support to the US Navy Sixth Fleet patrolling the Mediterranean and providing support to US interests after World War II. I heard that the Sixth Fleet in the Mediterranean might have now replaced the Seventh Fleet.

The cruise was for six months in duration before another marine battalion would relieve it. I was very interested in being on this cruise, but you had to have six months minimum remaining on your enlistment when the cruise departed. Therefore, after much thought, I extended my enlistment for three months and remained with my unit for the cruise. This really was not a difficult decision because I liked serving in the Marine Corps, and I had heard from marines who had been on the cruise that it was very interesting and worthwhile. I bet Leroy would have liked to have had this opportunity.

This was an exciting time. We had to pack all of our personal belongings, uniforms, and gear to accompany us on the cruise. In addition, all of our company administrative records and equipment were included on the cruise. Anyone having a need to take leave had to do so and return before mid-January 1957. We had to undergo several inspections to make sure that we were prepared with adequate clothing, that we were in proper physical condition, and that our weapons were in top-notch condition to support whatever situation we might encounter. All of our medical conditions had to be in order before departure.

The day finally arrived when we boarded the bus for Moorhead City where we met our ship that would be home for the next six months or so. Fortunately, this was a troop ship as opposed to a LST, whereby we would be landing from landing craft as opposed to AMTRACS. We all welcomed this type of ship. Once on board and settled in we received instructions on our daily routines. This amounted to calisthenics because we had to stay in physical shape as best we could for maneuvers. We also had classroom instructions, working party duty on the ship, and were always busy cleaning weapons. This would keep us busy. They knew that they should never leave marines with too much idle time for fear of what may happen.

We left Moorhead City on our way to the Rock of Gibraltar, which was our entry to the Mediterranean Sea. It took about six days at sea to reach Gibraltar. During this time, everything proceeded as planned. We were to spend three days in Gibraltar before performing our first amphibious maneuver. Once arriving at Gibraltar, we took turns on going on liberty. This was an interesting place to tour with all of its European-type settings. There were Barbary Macaques (tailless monkeys) in various parts of the city. In addition, there were British troops stationed there. There were also "ladies of the night" occupying the bars. Based upon what I was taught in religious classes to not have sexual activity outside of wedlock and therefore I did not patronize the prostitutes. We did not have reason to suspect this at the time, but these same prostitutes were at every port that our amphibious task force visited. How they knew the ports that we were to visit is beyond me, but they were there.

We were getting along pretty well with the British troops at the bars until one proposed a toast, "to the queen." A marine from another company and ship said, "F*** the queen," and all hell broke loose. One would think that US citizens would know that the British have great, great respect for their queen. Evidently, this marine did not get the word. I fortunately got out of the way in time. The shore patrol broke up the brawl and took a couple of marines into custody. I never heard if they received some form of punishment, but I imagine they did. This kind of behavior was not acceptable anywhere, but especially not in a foreign country. My friends and I returned to the ship without incident. Because of this incident, they instructed us on how to act in a foreign country.

Now we were back to sea. Our next stop was an amphibious maneuver in Sardinia. We did all of the preparations for the landing, making sure that all of the required materials were in place, such as rope to lash the mortars, and guide the mortars descending the ship into the landing craft without banging against the ship. We descended the ship using the nets. The physical landing went quite well, especially with calm seas. While running our maneuvers on land, some of the native Sardinians would try to sell some of their wares to us. I did buy an aluminum cup from one person, knowing that they probably needed the money. In fact, some sixty years later, I still have that cup. We never had the opportunity to go ashore on liberty in Sardinia and probably missed some good dining. I feel sure that there would have been some exciting tours and restaurants serving good Italian food had we had the opportunity to visit. However, the maneuver was over in a day and we were back on ship.

Our next stop was a port call in Naples, Italy. We were going to be there for nearly a week. Therefore, we had the opportunity to go on tours to various cities in Italy. I chose to visit Rome on a two-day tour. We rode the train to Rome. Once there we had a guided tour to see the main attractions in Rome and I am sure that we only hit the highlights due to the short stay. Rome was a very exciting city. We stayed overnight at the Hotel Medici, which was quite a treat from the troop ship accommodations. The food was also great compared to what we had on the ship.

One of the main attractions for me was to see Pope Pius XII at the Vatican. To me this was worth the three-month extension on my enlistment. I am sure that my classmates from Saints Peter & Paul High School, Waterloo, Illinois, would be quite envious of me, especially my buddy Leroy, knowing that I had the opportunity to see the Pope. We were able to tour St. Peter's Basilica and the Sistine Chapel. The Swiss guards with their colorful uniforms were very interesting. It was difficult to absorb all of the history of Rome and the Vatican in such a short time. It was a once-in-a-lifetime experience to see paintings by famous painters like Leonardo da Vinci.

Upon completion of the tour, we returned to the ship in Naples by train. I also had the opportunity to tour Naples, which are a beautiful city with its lavish royal palace and the large cathedral with all of the statues.

We were now back at sea. Our next stop was an amphibious landing maneuver on the Island of Crete, which is part of Greece and is its largest island. The preparations for landing and the actual landing were becoming routine for us. The old saying that practice makes perfect must have been taking effect. Our teamwork was really paying off.

The landing and the infantry maneuvers went quite well. During the maneuvers, several local people of Crete visited us. Our communication was poor. We could not speak Greek, and they could not speak English. We did the best we could to display good relations. We never had a liberty call in Crete, but I am sure it would have been most interesting. When the maneuvers were completed, we went aboard the landing craft and cruised back to the ship to climb the nets for boarding.

Back at sea, I was in charge of a working party to chip paint on the bow of the ship. Normally, they put corporals in charge of these types of details. While doing this working party, our company top sergeant informed me that I am now a sergeant. What a shocker! I did not know that they were considering me for promotion to sergeant. This really made me happy. I was not even thinking about being a sergeant on my current enlistment. This meant a few more dollars in my pocket. My monthly pay was now $140.40. In addition, when we returned to the states, I would be able to straggle to chow instead of marching in formation. What a surprise!

Now, I was seriously considering buying the Omega watch on display at the ship's store. These Omega watches are beautiful gold with handsome gold watchbands. The price for the watch was seventy-five dollars, which was a lot of money in those days. I did not have that much money, so I kept on dreaming. In later years, the "Omega Watch" story became a joke between my wife and me. She would ask me what I wanted for my birthday or Christmas, and I would tell her an Omega watch as a joke. This went on for more than fifty years, and lo' and behold, she presented me with an Omega watch for my seventy-fifth birthday! I know that she had to pay a lot more than seventy-five dollars in today's economy. In fact, that Omega watch is so nice that I am afraid to wear it except for special occasions like weddings.

Living on a troop ship for these many months required the use of ingenuity to maintain our utility uniforms, now referred to as "camos," meaning camouflaged uniforms in today's military. Back then, the utility uniforms were not camouflaged and simply solid green in color. There were no timely laundry services available aboard ship. Our laundry had to be by hand for the most part. Some marines would tie their utility uniforms to a rope and throw them overboard to for washing by the ocean while the ship was moving. This not only washed the uniforms, but the salt water would fade the coloring. Marines liked this because it made them look salty and provided a false sense of seniority. This technique went well for a while until the sailors started cutting the ropes that were unattended. You would think that this would have caused a riot, but it did not because the marines knew they were probably in the wrong. This washing technique did not stop. However, we watched the ropes very closely from then on.

Our next stop was a port call in Istanbul, Turkey. This was a history-rich city to tour. Nothing eventful occurred at this stop other than an interesting tour of Istanbul. This city is huge and so full of history. The Topkapi Palace was one of the major residences of the Ottoman sultans for almost 400 of their 624-year reign. Any history buff could have had a field day here in Istanbul.

Because some marines and sailors could not resist the women of the night, our corpsmen would occasionally hold reveille at 0500, line up everyone without going to the head, and check us for venereal disease. I did not know anyone that had the disease, but if they did, they would be required to go to sick call for treatment. These corpsmen did not hesitate to report to the CO anyone that gave them a hard time. They were really looking out for our best interest and we appreciated their efforts, even though marines sometimes did not show it outwardly.

A few days after leaving Istanbul, we conducted another amphibious landing in Turkey not far from Istanbul. Again, we ran the normal infantry maneuvers. The landing and the infantry maneuvers went well. As usual, the local Turks visited us trying to sell their wares. We had the normal language barrier.

However, we again did the best we could to display good relations as US citizens.

It was now Easter weekend when we arrived at Genoa, Italy. We were to be there for a week. Several of the marines took advantage of the various tours that they offered. I elected to stay in port and tour Genoa. Genoa is a beautiful city to tour, with such points of interest as the Genoa Cathedral.

However, early Easter Monday morning around 0500, I heard an enormous racket. They were loading the vehicles back aboard the ship. Whenever we were in port for a few days, they unloaded some vehicles for the various shore duty functions such as shore patrol. I could not understand why this was happening this early. I had no idea what was going on. There were several marines on tours. I found out that we were going to be underway by noon that day. No one seemed to know and the top brass was not talking. The fastest ship in our amphibious task force would remain behind to pick up those on tour and catch up with their home ships later. None of us remaining on the ship knew what was going on.

Something was happening very quickly that we knew nothing about. Early that afternoon, when we were underway, the word came down to gather at the fantail of the ship with our personal weapons to test fire and make sure they were operational, which we did. We had to be preparing for combat. Everything seemed to be in order. Next, we had to double up on our bunks. You would sleep for eight hours, and then your friend would sleep for eight hours. The reason for this was that they were clearing out berthing areas on the ship, why no one knew this was going to happen was beyond me. The operational plans development must have been in process as events unfolded.

Then we got the word that we were on our way to Beirut, Lebanon, to evacuate American citizens. Now we knew why we were vacating the berthing areas and why we had to test fire our weapons. We were also awaiting word on what we were to do when we landed. What were the rules of engagement going to be and other details of this nature? We knew we had to protect the American citizens, but that was about all that we knew.

This was the closest I had to combat duty while in the marines. The day before this was to happen, we received word of restoring peace and they cancelled the evacuation. This was great news. However, we did not even know whom the enemy was that we were preparing to fight. We did get to go ashore in Beirut on liberty, which was enjoyable. Beirut, the capital of Lebanon, was a beautiful city. The national museum of Beirut was very interesting to tour. The cancellation of our evacuation mission made this liberty call very special. Subsequent war torn events, I am sure have deteriorated the once beauty of Beirut.

Our next port of call was Corfu, Greece. The seasonal time to change uniforms going from winter to summer had arrived. Our company top tasked me to negotiate with the local people to have our khaki uniforms laundered and pressed. I suppose that because of my recent promotion to sergeant, they wanted to test my negotiating skills much less my linguist talent. This was not an easy task. I could not speak Greek, and I doubted if I could find anyone in Corfu that could speak English. However, I was going to try.

I went to a few laundries and cleaners without success because of the language barrier. Then, at a bar, someone introduced me to a person from Chicago who was now living in Corfu. We hit it off fairly well. He seemed happy to carry on a conversation in English. I was lucky. I told him what I was after, and he took me to the place to have the laundry done at a fair price. He and I made all of the arrangements for the logistics of having the uniforms picked up, laundered, and delivered in our specified timeframe. I really got an appreciation for the citizens in Corfu because of this tasking. When we got the uniforms back, everyone seemed happy. I am not sure, but my fellow marines probably thought I was fluent in Greek languish. They were really in for a surprise!

Izmir, Turkey was our next port to visit. This was an interesting city to visit, but nothing out of the ordinary occurred. I went on an abbreviated tour of Izmir. There was a lot to see, but you can only see so much in a one-day liberty call. The museums, statues, and churches in Izmir were very interesting to see. Izmir is the third most populated city in Turkey. This was only a two-day port call, and then we were back at sea. We then had an amphibious landing and infantry maneuver near Izmir for another two days.

Our next stop was Rhodes, Greece. This was another real exciting place to visit. My friends got the impression from my negotiating experience in Corfu that I was a superior Greek linguist. How wrong they were. We toured this island, which was full of historic places. Old town Rhodes with the cobblestone streets dated back to the crusades. I also had the opportunity to taste ouzo for the first time, which was quite an experience. Ouzo is some powerful stuff. A few of the marines tasted a little too much ouzo and resulted in having to be escorted back to the ship. Fortunately, I knew when I had had enough ouzo and had sense enough to quit.

Our Mediterranean cruise was nearing an end. We were to stop at Malaga, Spain, for a few days, and then Gibraltar for a day or so, and then across the ocean back to Moorhead City. Malaga was another interesting city to visit and full of history. Malaga is one of the oldest cities in the world, dating back over 2,800 years. I had the opportunity to see a bullfight, which was a little gruesome but interesting. The matadors were a real spectacle. I knew that I would probably never have the opportunity to see a bull fight in the United States.

Our final stop was Gibraltar. Being there for the second time gave us a chance to further visit additional sites now that we were a little more familiar with the area. Many of us did take advantage of dining at good restaurants. The food aboard ship was good, but some of us felt that we needed a change. I am not sure if the marines that caused the brawl with their inflammatory comment about the queen of England in front of the British soldiers were authorized liberty on this port call. As far as I knew, everyone behaved, and we left without incident.

Crossing the ocean gave us time to think of what we experienced the past several months in the Mediterranean. This was a lot to absorb. Without a doubt, it was well worth the three-month extension to my enlistment. This was late June 1957. In a little over two months, my enlistment would be up. What am I going to do now? I could reenlist, but I was not planning to, even though I did enjoy being in the Corps. I put the decision of my future on hold because I had a couple of months to think about what to do.

Arriving at Moorhead City was quite an experience. Several of the wives and girlfriends of my fellow marines were on the dock to greet their loved ones. As we walked down the gangplank, we heard Elvis Presley singing "Hound Dog" for the first time. This was my first exposure to Elvis Presley but definitely not my last. Everyone was in a festive mood. We then boarded the bus and were on our way back to Camp Lejeune. I was having mixed feelings on our way to Camp Lejeune. On one hand, I was happy to be back, but on the other hand, I was sort of missing the Mediterranean.

Because I only had a little over two months left to serve on my enlistment, I was reassigned to a staging area in the Sixth Marines headquarter area. I was fortunate to be with the same unit for my entire enlistment after boot camp until now. There, I received a physical and a dental exam. I had to make appointments for some dental work. This was required as part of being released from active duty. I was in charge of working parties to police the area and to do various housekeeping chores of this nature.

In addition, while there, they gave me the reenlistment sales pitch. They made me a potential attractive offer that involved sending me to preparatory school. This would be a preliminary step for entrance to the Naval Academy at Annapolis, Maryland. Providing I completed the preparatory school satisfactorily, I then had the opportunity to enter the Naval Academy. After four years, I would graduate with a degree in engineering and a commission as a second lieutenant in the Marine Corps or as an ensign in the Navy. Then, I would have four more years to serve on active duty. This sounded very good, but I declined because of too many "ifs." There were other alternatives offered for me to think about, but I declined them all. The main reason that I declined reenlistment was because I felt that I needed a change and wanted to try out civilian life. Keep in mind; I had very little exposure to civilian life after high school. If civilian life did not work out, I could always enlist again in the Corps.

September 7, 1957, finally arrived. They officially released me from active duty and I received my DD Form 214. This is the official document showing that you served. My friend from Louisiana who was married was released at the same time. He and his wife volunteered to drive me home to Renault, Illinois for which I was most grateful. I stayed in contact with my Louisiana friends over the years. My high school friend Leroy did not serve in the military. He stayed in the Waterloo area and worked for various employers.

This concluded my tour in the military. You see, it was not too bad after all. My intention was to give you a first-hand account of my experience in the military in hopes that it will help you in deciding what to do after graduation from high school.

Chapter 9

RETURN TO RENAULT

Arriving home as a civilian was great. My parents, relatives, and friends welcomed me home with all of the pleasantries one could expect.

After three years and three months in the military, it left me wondering how to best adjust to civilian life. Now I had to think about getting a job in hopes that I could later go to school on the GI Bill. I suppose that I could have taken a few weeks to acclimate myself to civilian life, but I did not. I have always been the type of person to proceed with what needed to done in an expeditious manner. I have a type "A" personality.

I went to the unemployment office in St. Louis, Missouri, and I told them that I wanted an office job because after three years in the infantry, I had had enough of physical work and outdoor living. Please do not get the idea that was lazy. They found me a job with a government contractor as a mail clerk, which was fine. All I had to do was to pick up the mail from the post office that was about six blocks from our office twice a day. In addition, I had to type inventory cards for the source documentation being sent to the home office in Springfield Massachusetts, where they were writing technical manuals for the army. I was never good at typing even in high school, but I struggled through this assignment. I sometimes wondered why my typing teacher in high school, Sister Stevens gave me a passing grade.

Now, I thought, I needed a car. With the small amount that I had saved with bonds while in the marines, I had enough for a down payment to buy a new 1957 Ford "Fairlane". This really made me feel like a big shot. Maybe now I could attract the girls without the marine dress blue uniform. The car only cost me $2,700 back then. A similar car now would probably cost around $27,000.

I then signed up to go to night school, learning about diesel mechanics. I thought that with a little luck, I might be able to land a job with a trucking company maintaining those big rigs. Little did I know at the time that this diesel mechanics school really turned out to be the key to my future by giving me the mechanical training needed to pursue potential advancement as an equipment specialist?

About a month after returning home, I received a notice from the draft board saying that I was delinquent in registering for the draft, which I was.

Of course, they piled on the penalties that I would receive if I did not report.

I had enlisted in the Marine Corps at age seventeen, and you did not have to register for the draft until age eighteen. While in the marines, I never thought once about the draft. Now, with the threat of penalties, I visited the draft board, showed them my DD Form 214, which is the official record of service, and all was forgiven. Instead of criminal treatment, they rather treated me as a hero. That was a real relief for me. I could picture myself inducted into the army for another couple of years of service. My high school friend Leroy would then have had the last laugh.

After a few months of working and going to diesel mechanics school, my boss who seemed to care about my future and told me that he was going to promote me to junior equipment specialist. The diesel mechanics school was the reason for this. He and I use to shoot the breeze about cars and general mechanics. He assigned me to work with a senior equipment specialist, which turned out to be great. I did not know then that this was the stepping-stone to my career, which all hinged on diesel mechanics school and teamwork and discipline training from the marines.

About three months later, the company that initially employed me lost the contract. The winning company employed me as a junior technical writer developing parts manuals for the army. This really opened my eyes to defense contracting.

I then met this young woman, Bessie who became my wonderful wife on July 11, 1959. This really gave me the sense of responsibility to provide for the well-being of a family. We have now celebrated fifty-seven years of marriage and have four daughters, nine grandchildren, and eight great-grandchildren. Bessie really was a key to my success by keeping me on the right path when it came to decision making about our future.

About two years after I got married, I accepted a job as a technical writer on the Titan I Inter-Continental Ballistic Missile (ICBM) System in Denver, Colorado. Initially, a friend from the office and I had seen an ad in the *St. Louis Post Dispatch* for technical writers, and we responded to the ad and scheduled an interview. During the interview, we indicated that our salary requirements were twice our current salary. When we returned home from the interview, we were laughing about our salary requirement and said that we would never hear from that recruiter again. Lo' and behold, about an hour after returning home from the interview, the recruiter phoned and asked us how soon could we be available to start to work in Denver on the Titan I ICBM System. Who in the world would have ever thought that this job offer would occur? We relocated to Denver, which was a very enjoyable assignment. In 1964, the Titan I program phased out and caused us to relocate back to the St. Louis area where I was accepted into federal civil service as a supply cataloger.

After a few years of service in the Federal Government, I volunteered to be part of an inventory group assembled by the US Army Materiel Command to spend six months in Vietnam setting up an inventory control program called Project Counter. This effort required teamwork. They put me in charge of a team to identify items and get then on location in the depot for issue. They named my team "Rickert's Raiders." Upon returning from Vietnam, I assisted the data processing group as a functional analyst in developing a new cataloging data module. Through this detail, they promoted me to a computer systems analyst position and I attended a few months of IBM school to learn the ropes in data processing.

After a few more years, I received another promotion for an assignment in Battle Creek, Michigan, as the army representative in developing the Defense Integrated Data System (DIDS). Battle Creek was the cereal capital of the world and an interesting city. This assignment required teamwork and coordination with the other military services and the Department of Defense. During this assignment, I had to work closely with a senior executive at the Army Materiel Command in Alexandria, Virginia. Through this relationship, I received another promotion and relocation to Headquarters, Army Materiel Command in Alexandria, VA as a supply specialist. We decided to live in southern Maryland, and I would commute to Alexandria.

Soon after my relocation to Alexandria, I was faced with a reorganization of the Army Materiel Command whereby they were decentralizing some headquarter functions to field activities. In my case, they were considering transferring my cataloging functions to the Cataloging Data Activity located at New Cumberland, Pennsylvania. I opposed such a transfer because I did not want to put my family through another geographic relocation in such a short time. I was especially concerned with three of my daughters who were in school. My concern leads me to consider the possibility of a career change and leaving the federal government.

Fortunately, they spared me from having to relocate to Pennsylvania and enabled me to continue my career in federal service. However, this caused me to think about having a fallback position if confronted with a similar situation in the future. I suggested to Bessie that we consider training for the real estate industry as a backup. She agreed, and we then contacted a real estate broker to find out what we needed to do to get started. This required us to enroll in a real estate class at the community college. This turned out to be very interesting, and upon the completion of the course, we took the State of Maryland Real Estate Exam and successfully passed. We then went back to the broker and became part of his sales staff. I was part time, and Bessie was full time. This turned out to be a very interesting endeavor that was also financially rewarding.

Because of this relocation to the job in Alexandria, we bought a home in southern Maryland, from where I commuted to Alexandria for the next fourteen years. I then retired from federal service, and we decided to stay in southern Maryland as opposed to retiring to Florida, North Carolina, or some other location common to retirees. In addition, at this point, we had four daughters with husbands and five grandchildren. To get Bessie to move away from her grandchildren would have been next to impossible.

I was only fifty-one years old when I retired from federal service on an early retirement (early out), and as a result, I worked for defense contractors for the next twenty-five years when I retired for good. I am fortunate to remain in good health. I am also enjoying retirement at age eighty.

EPILOGUE

My whole purpose of writing this book was to tell my story of what I experienced in transitioning from a seventeen-year-old farm boy to a mature twenty-year-old citizen pursuing a career. Little did I know at the time that the military tour opened my eyes to new horizons in thinking and in determining my career path?

It seems that today, more than ever, young people have difficulty in selecting a career path after high school, or in some cases, even after college. Thanks to the Marine Corps, where they instilled in my mind the discipline and teamwork required for success. I learned how to maintain a way of life on my own without having to rely completely on others. This was a valuable experience for me.

Had it not been for this experience, I probably would not have made the decisions I made in pursuing my career the way that I did. In laying out what actually happened in my three-plus years in the Marine Corps, I hope to help others in deciding if they want to proceed down a similar road. True, I had some luck along the way, but I also took risks. It is like the old adage, "you can't win the lottery if you don't buy a chance,". I took the chance, and my wife and I feel that we came out winners in the end. In addition, the brief synopsis of my life after leaving the Marine Corps may help others to decide if they wanted to pursue a similar career path where mobility is important.

I feel that my career has been successful for many reasons, starting with my parents raising me to work hard, obey the law, maintain the spiritual beliefs, and to respect others. High school played an important role in providing proper learning techniques, behavior, and respect for authority, in addition to instilling the need for spiritual wisdom. Lastly, the Marine Corps played an important role in my future. The discipline, chain of command authority, love of country, loyalty, physical fitness, teamwork, and the motto, semper fidelis, learned during my military service were positives in shaping my career.

There have been many changes in the current way of life as compared to the way it was sixty years ago. Today, we have improved communications that were unheard of in my youth. Today has sophisticated telephone systems, information technology systems, social media, transportation systems, and the increased level of education, which has certainly changed the way of life, as we knew it back then.

The employment then was much more reliable than today. Manufacturing was booming and so was employment. Everyone then could find employment if they were physically and mentally able. Some employees back then could make a career with one organization. Today, this is not the case. The reason is that many of the jobs have moved to other countries outside the United States, and automation has replaced many manual jobs. Now, more than ever, education and specialized training become necessary in securing employment.

Back then only, a few people went to college, which normally was for the wealthy and upper-middle class. High school back then was equivalent for the most part to a college degree in today's world from a numbers perspective. Social changes have also occurred during this period. Racial relations have also improved, even though we need further improvement. The military now is an all-volunteer military because of the discontinuance of the draft. Military men and women are now serving together more closely, which was unheard of back then.

Problems have also intensified during this time. Drug problems are much more prevalent today than they were back then, as an example. Back then, alcohol abuse was the problem and still is today, but not to the extent that drugs are today. Crime has also seemed to be on the rise. The threat of terrorism at home is with us now, which we hardly heard of sixty years ago. These are only a few things that have influenced the way of life, as we know it today.

What has not changed is the fact that there continues to be high school graduates and some college graduates who do not know what to do after graduation. The intent of this book is to show that there is a path forward. That path can move you forward to a successful career. In no way am I advocating the discontinuance of education after high school. What I am saying is that rather than accepting a job working in an unhappy environment the remainder of your life; why not consider something more adventurous? Maybe the door to your thinking can be opened and provide additional insight to your thinking.

Many people now know little about military life. Most parents today did not serve in the military. Therefore, their children did not hear military stories and experiences from parents. All that they hear about the military is from news programs where they report on wounded and deaths for the most part. This is why I felt that a detail description of my experience in the Marine Corps could help clarify any misconceptions about the military. This combined with a summary of my career experience after my military service may shed some light on deciding what to do after high school graduation. By no means am I advocating that you should join the marines. There are similar paths in the other military services, and there are the Peace Corps and other organizations that can provide the starting point for overcoming this problem of what to do after high school or college graduation. The point is that you would benefit in considering all options before deciding.

I am hoping that this book will assist you and others in choosing a way of life that takes advantage of what our country has to offer and stay on a positive track for success.

Andrew J. Rickert was raised on a farm in Renault, Illinois, and joined the US Marine Corps at age seventeen, in 1954. After three years, he returned to civilian life and found success in several different fields. Now retired, he and his wife live in Maryland.

This book is the author's actual experience obtaining a career path after graduating from high school. This seventeen-year-old individual raised on a farm in Renault, Illinois, enlisted in the Marine Corps, which became the stepping-stone to his career in civilian life.

Printed in the United States
By Bookmasters